HANDS-ON LEARNING DRILLS FOR SOUNDS

SCIENCE EXPERIMENTS FOR KIDS
CHILDREN'S SCIENCE EDUCATION BOOKS

Speedy Publishing LLC

40 E. Main St. #1156

Newark, DE 19711

www.speedypublishing.com

Copyright 2017

In this book, we're going to talk about sounds and some simple sound experiments you can do at home or school. Make sure an adult is there to help you so you're safe when conducting experiments. So, let's get right to it!

WHAT IS SOUND?

You hear your mom calling you for dinner from the kitchen. The school bell rings and that means you'll be moving to the next class. You hold your kitten and she makes a purring sound. Sound travels through the air. Your ears can hear the sounds and then your brain interprets what they mean.

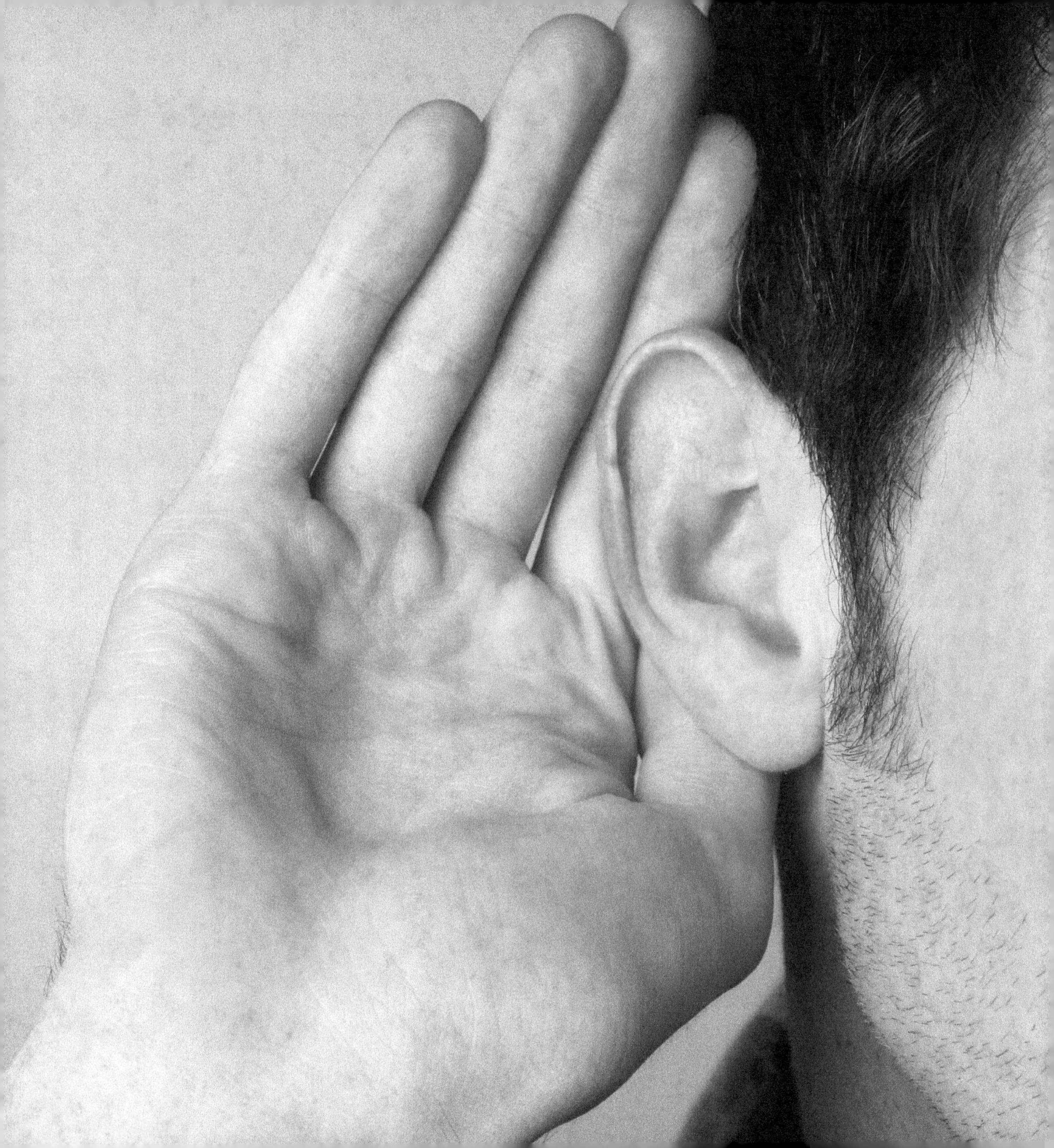

SOUND WAVE

Sound is composed of waves that can travel through different forms of matter. Waves of sound can travel through air and they can also travel through water. In fact, they travel four times faster in water than they do in air!

HOW DOES SOUND MOVE?

A sound starts when something mechanical happens. For example, let's say you knock on a door. The molecules where you hit the door begin to vibrate and since sound is a wave it causes molecules around those molecules to vibrate as well.

GIRL KNOCKING

A YOUNG WOMAN ANSWERING THE DOOR

Depending on how hard you knocked on the door, someone in the back of the house might not be able to hear the sound. The waves of sound travel from the mechanical event through the air to reach someone's ears.

WHAT IS THE SPEED OF SOUND?

The speed that sound travels through different types of matter can be calculated. In air that isn't too humid it travels about 767 miles per hour, but it varies depending on atmospheric conditions and temperature.

TEMPERATURE

ASTRONAUT IN OUTER SPACE

ARE THERE SOUNDS IN SPACE?

Unlike light, which moves the fastest when it travels through a vacuum, sounds can't be heard in a vacuum at all. This means that if you were in outer space just floating around you couldn't call out for help. In order for sound waves to travel they have to be able to vibrate matter. If there's no matter there, they can't travel.

It's a good thing there is a way for astronauts to talk to each other in space. They have devices in their helmets that are able to transfer the sound waves created by their voices into waves that are transmitted by radio signals.

SPACE HELMET

RADIO WAVE

Radio waves aren't the same as sound waves. They are a type of electromagnetic radiation that is similar to light so they can move in a vacuum, unlike sound.

EXPERIMENT 1

DO-IT-YOURSELF GONG

To do this experiment, you'll need a few items. You'll need a fairly heavy 1-foot long wooden or plastic ruler. You'll also need a regular teaspoon, larger serving spoon, and a serving fork. About 4 feet of either string or yarn will be the last thing you need. You may need to adjust the string or yarn depending on your height.

GONG

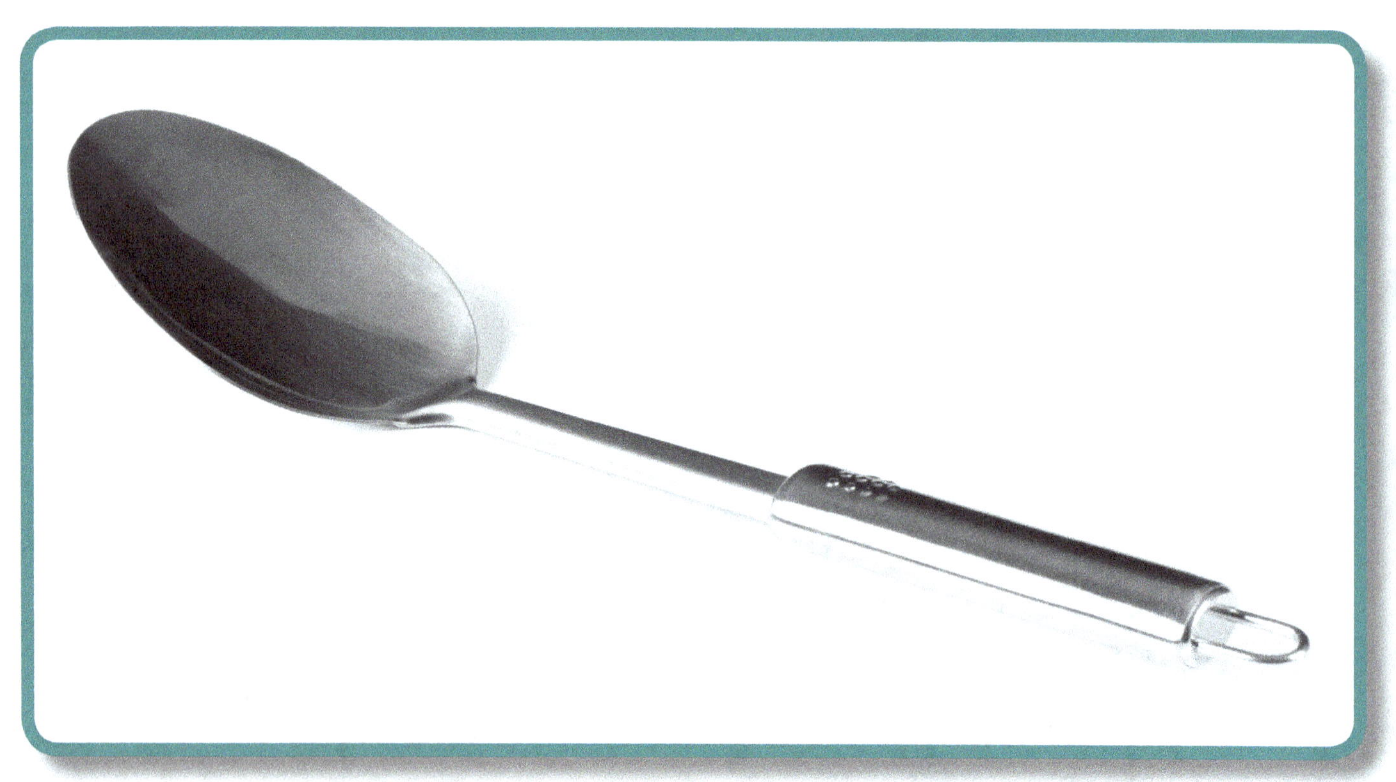

LARGER SERVING SPOON

DO THE EXPERIMENT

Make a loop in the center point of your string or yarn and insert the handle of the larger serving spoon. Tie the yarn tightly so the spoon hangs in the center and you have an equal amount of string on each side, just as if you were making a spoon necklace. Now take the ends of the strings and wrap them around the pointer fingers on each of your hands.

Now push the string against each ear. You shouldn't put the yarn into your ears just against the outside of them. The spoon should be hanging with its handle closest to your face and its spoon head pointing toward the floor. The spoon handle should be close to your waist, if it isn't you may need more yarn if you're taller!

YARN

TEASPOON

Now that you're ready, have someone else gently strike the ruler on the round part of the spoon. You'll hear a gong-like sound.

With your experiment set up, it's time to try some different things. Try the small spoon instead of the larger spoon and hear what happens. This spoon will sound more bell-like than the larger spoon.

Try moving up the yarn on both sides so instead of having the end pieces of the yarn to your ears you have each side 6 inches or 12 inches down on each side. Try a serving fork instead of the spoons. Try hitting the spoons or forks at different levels of intensity to see how it changes the sound.

WOODEN RULER

FORK

Other people who are in the room will hear the sound from the spoons being hit, but they won't hear the louder gong-like or bell-like sounds that are traveling through the string or yarn.

SCIENTIFIC EXPLANATION

When the person strikes the ruler against the spoon, it's a mechanical activity that creates waves of sound. The waves travel up the attached yarn or string and to your ears instead of diffusing into the surrounding air. This happens because the string or yarn is conducting the sound waves and giving them someplace to travel.

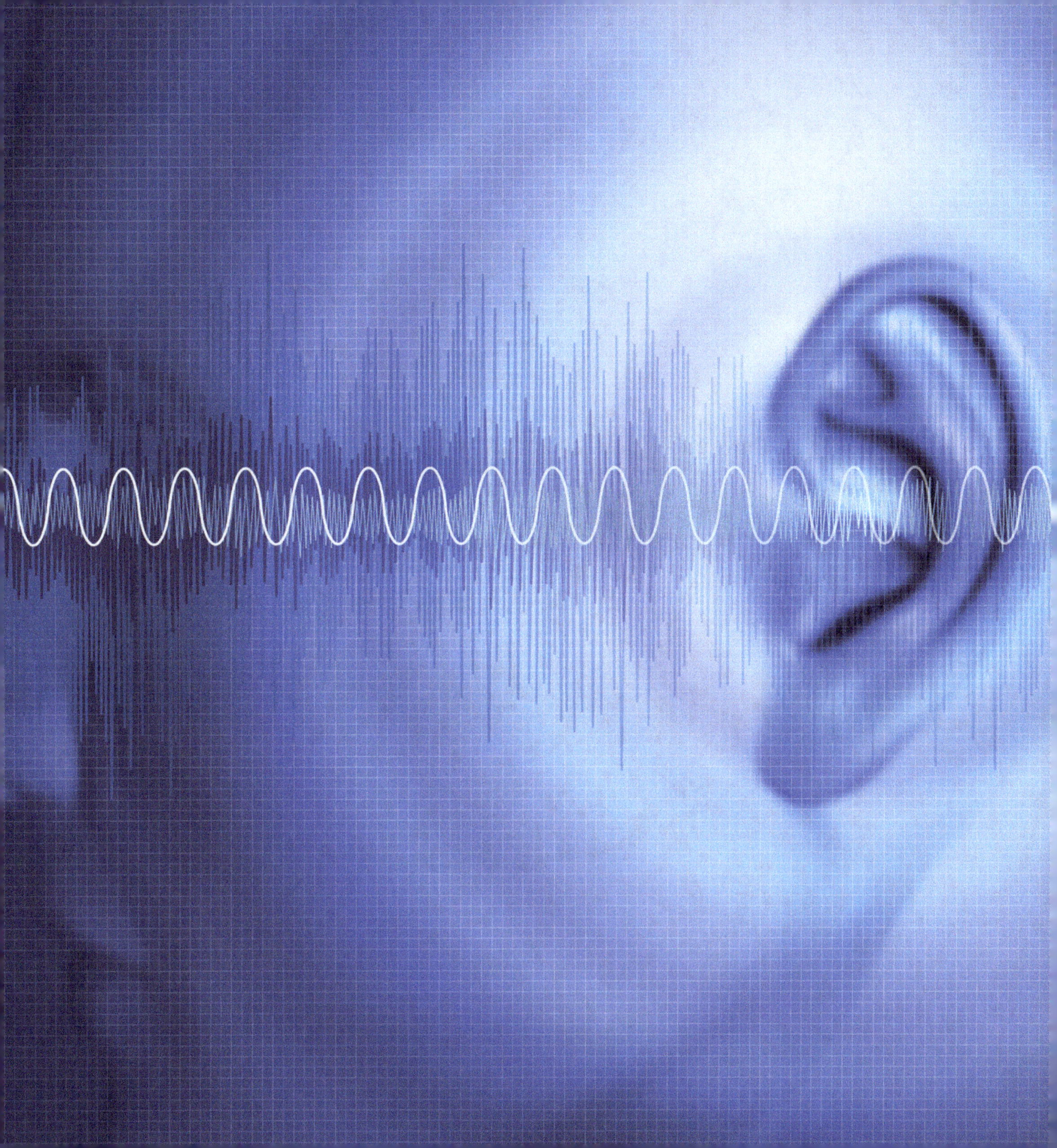

STRING

The string or yarn is a conductor of sound. Depending on the type of utensil you use and the size of the utensil, the sound will vary. The length of the yarn will make a difference in the sound you hear as well. If you try different types of string you will also notice that the denser the string is, the better it will conduct the sound.

EXPERIMENT 2

STAR WARS SLINKY

To do this experiment, you'll need a strong Styrofoam cup and a metal slinky. A plastic slinky won't work so make sure it's a metal one.

METAL SLINKY TOY

STYROFOAM CUPS

DO THE EXPERIMENT

Push the end piece of the slinky through the cup's base. Make sure it's in there securely. Hold the cup away from your body and dangle the slinky so it's hanging toward the floor. Now, gently move the cup from left to right and back again. You should hear sounds that are similar to the sounds heard in the movie Star Wars. Try moving the cup up and down to get a different type of sound.

SCIENTIFIC EXPLANATION

As the slinky moves, the sound vibrations are moving up the slinky into the cup. Then, the cup also vibrates, which causes part of the sound you hear. As you move the slinky from side to side or up and down the sound travels.

KID PLAYING WITH SLINKY

VIBRATION

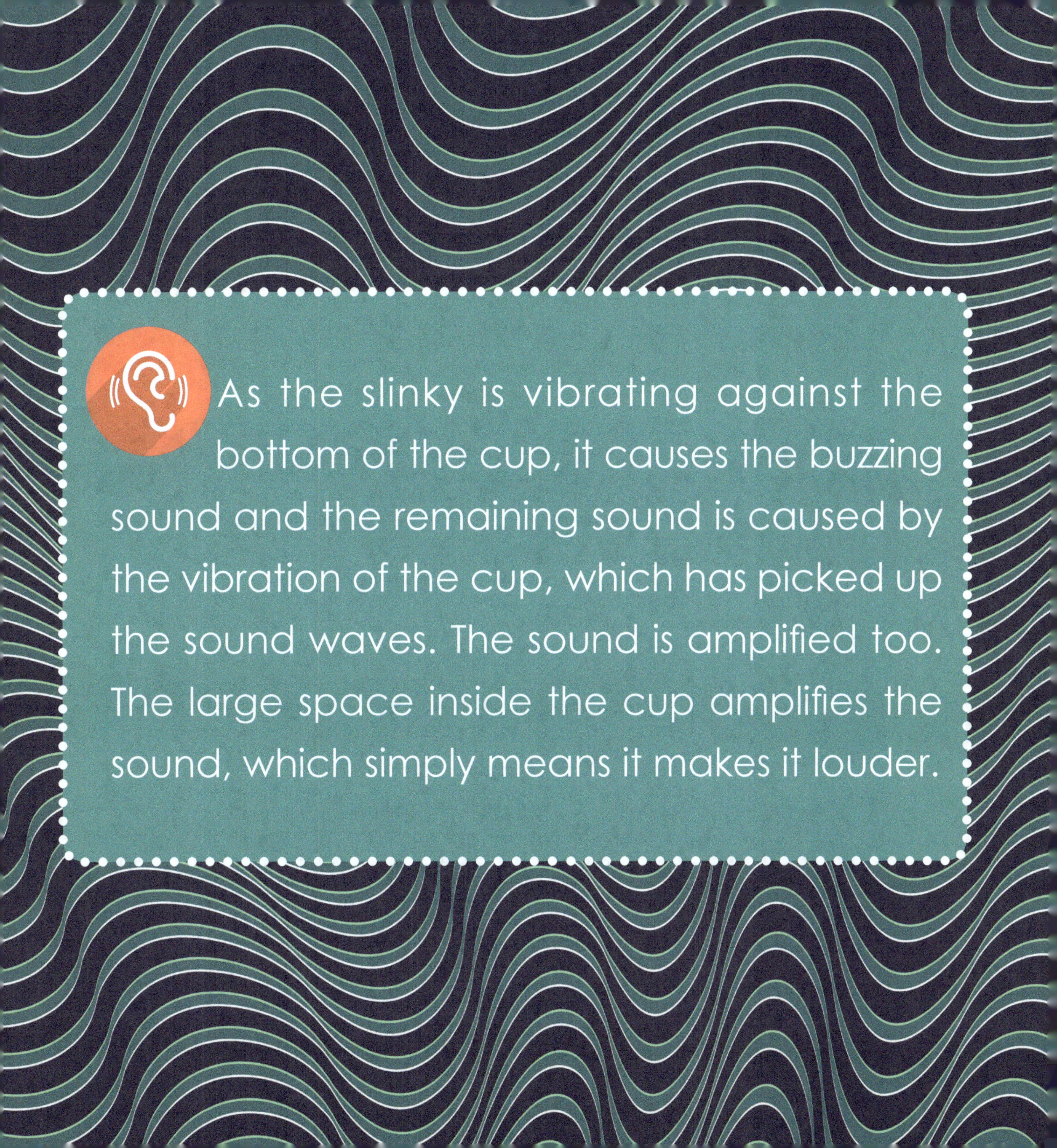
As the slinky is vibrating against the bottom of the cup, it causes the buzzing sound and the remaining sound is caused by the vibration of the cup, which has picked up the sound waves. The sound is amplified too. The large space inside the cup amplifies the sound, which simply means it makes it louder.

EXPERIMENT 3

THE UNDERWATER TELEPHONE

To do this experiment, you'll need two small plastic funnels. You'll also need a long piece of rubber tubing that will fit over the ends of the funnels. Last you'll need a plastic balloon. Since the experiment takes place underwater, you'll need a backyard pool that's big enough to submerge in water. Make sure there's an adult supervising you.

FUNNELS

DO THE EXPERIMENT

Fit the ends of the funnels into the rubber tubing. Stretch the plastic balloon over the circular part of one of the funnels. Make sure that it's tightly stretched across. Put the funnel that has the balloon stretched over it underwater.

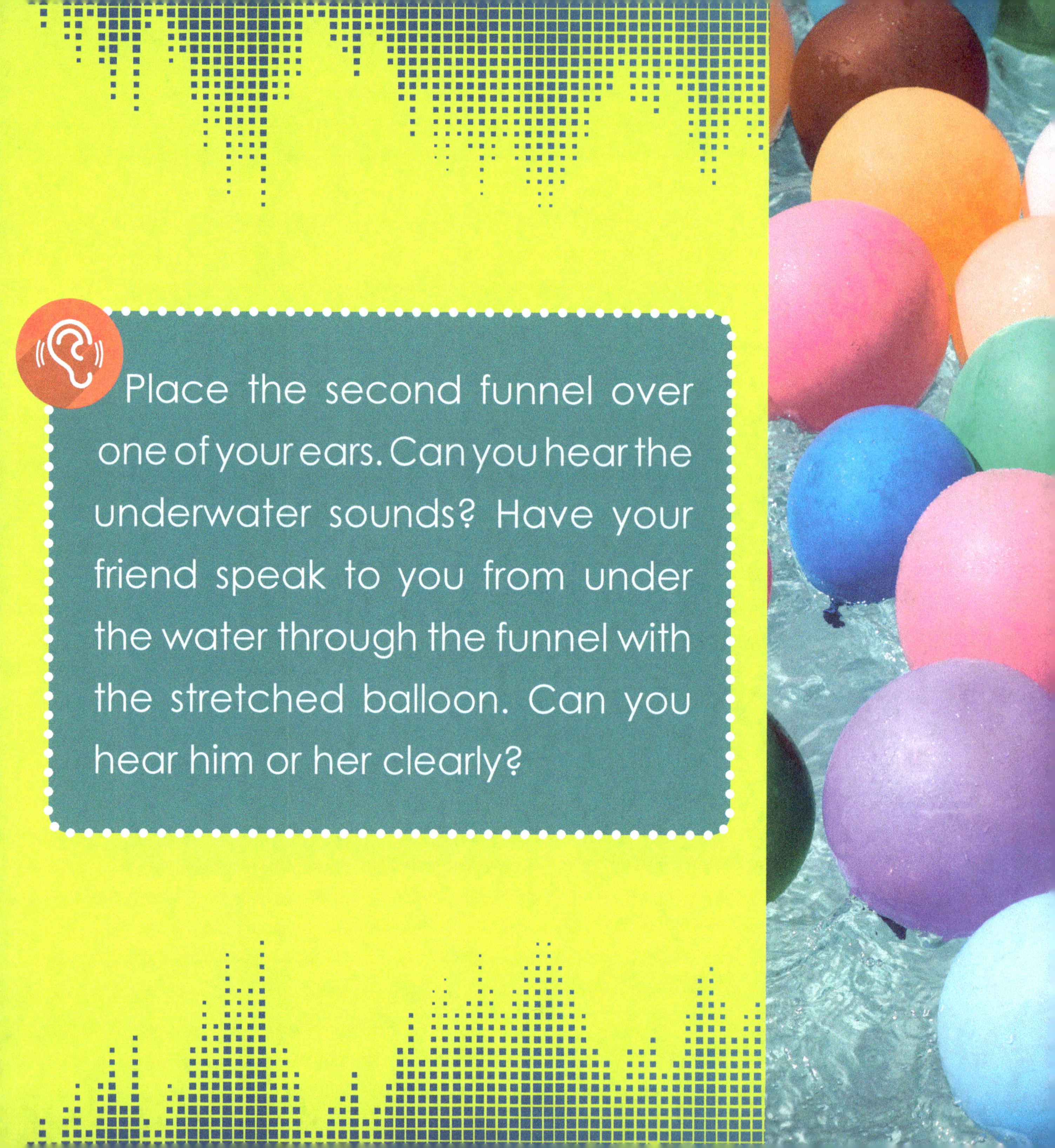

Place the second funnel over one of your ears. Can you hear the underwater sounds? Have your friend speak to you from under the water through the funnel with the stretched balloon. Can you hear him or her clearly?

BALLOONS FLOATING IN A SWIMMING POOL

HAPPY WHALE BREACHING

SCIENTIFIC EXPLANATION

Remember that sound is created by traveling vibrations. The funnel with the stretched balloon over it is able to pick up these sound waves as they travel through water. It also amplifies the sound and makes it louder so that you're able to hear it. Humpback whales sing songs under the ocean.

They can hear each many miles away because sound travels much faster in the water than it does in air. The reason is that the molecules in the water are packed together more tightly than the molecules of the different gases that make up Earth's air.

Sound can travel faster through water because it doesn't lose as much energy as it travels through water compared to when it travels through air.

CALF AND MOTHER HUMPBACK WHALES

BOY LISTENING TO MUSIC ON HEADPHONES

EXPERIMENT 4

"SEEING" SOUND WAVES

To do this experiment, you just need a few materials. You'll need a CD player or other music system with a speaker. You'll need some tissues and a needle and thread.

DO THE EXPERIMENT

Using a needle and thread, tie a piece of thread to a tissue. Hold the tissue from the thread in front of the speaker, a few inches away. Now turn on the music. The tissue should move when the music is played since invisible sound waves are hitting it as they leave the speaker. Try experimenting with different songs at different levels of volume and observe what happens to the tissue.

TISSUE

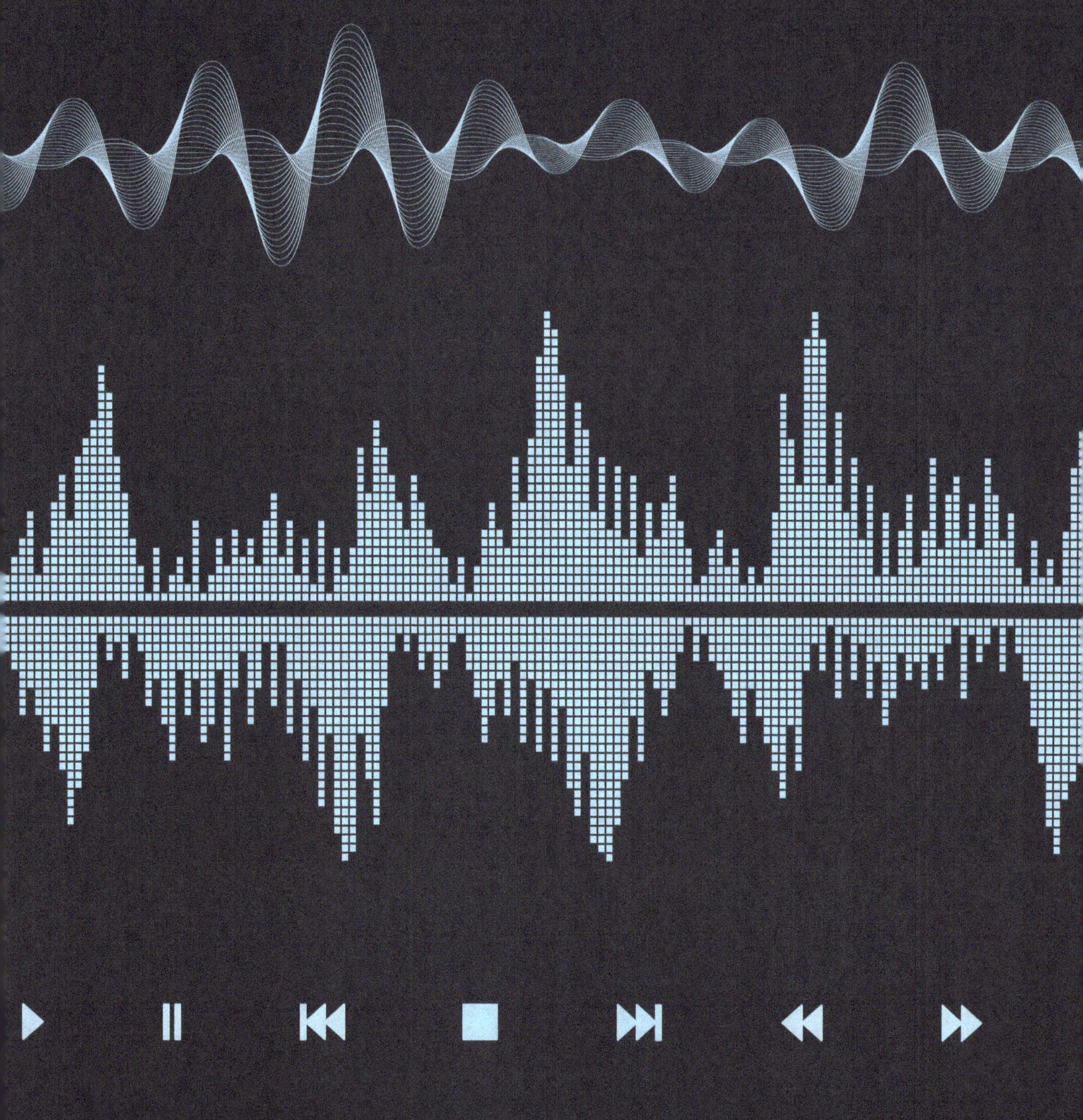

SCIENTIFIC EXPLANATION

Even though you can't see the invisible sound waves, you know they are there because the lightweight tissue moves in response to them. You're seeing the results of the waves in action.

Awesome! Now you know more about sound by doing your own experiments. You can find more Science Education books from Baby Professor by searching the website of your favorite book retailer.

Visit
BABY PROFESSOR
EDUCATION KIDS
www.BabyProfessorBooks.com
to download Free Baby Professor eBooks
and view our catalog of new and exciting
Children's Books